Table of Contents

Teacher's Annotated Pages

Table of Contents

Name _____

LANGUAGE AND USAGE

1 | What Is a Sentence?

▶ A **sentence** tells what someone or something does.

Grandma plants her garden.
The flowers bloom.

Write the word or words to finish each sentence.

★ <u>The sun</u> shines. **(The sun, Hot)**

1. Flowers _____ . **(red, bloom)**

2. _____ buzz. **(Bees, Jump)**

3. Birds _____ . **(trees, build nests)**

4. _____ turn green. **(Run, Leaves)**

5. Children _____ . **(play ball, flowers)**

6. _____ open windows. **(People, Big)**

Name _____

LANGUAGE AND USAGE

2 | Naming Part

▶ The **naming part** of a sentence tells whom or what a sentence is about.

The children bring pets to school.
Their show begins at noon.

Write the naming part to finish **each** sentence.

★ _____Ted_____ drops his frog, Bully.
   (Smiled, Ted)

1. _____ hops onto Mr. Pratt's head.
   (Bully, Moves)

2. _____ jumps in surprise.
   (Sits down, Mr. Pratt)

3. _____ falls into the box.
   (Blows away, His hat)

4. _____ covers the box.
   (The teacher, Stands)

5. _____ wins a prize.
   (The frog, Swims away)

3 | Action Part

> ► The **action part** of a sentence tells what is happening.
>
> The team **runs every day**.
> I **watch the track meet**.

Write the action part to finish each sentence.

★ The games **start at noon** .
(in the morning, start at noon)

1. Rosa _____ .
(on the track, runs short races)

2. Paul _____ .
(up and over again, jumps)

3. Ann _____ .
(runs long races, very short jumps)

4. Carlos _____ .
(throws a ball, heavy and round)

5. I _____ .
(my fast friends, cheer for them)

LANGUAGE AND USAGE

4 | Is It a Sentence?

▶ A sentence has a naming part and an action part.

naming part		action part
The baseball game	**+**	**begins.**

The baseball game begins.

Write **yes** beside each group of words that is a sentence.
Write **no** beside each group of words that is not a sentence.

★ Rico bats.   _yes_

1. the players   _____

2. The ball flies high.   _____

3. keeps running   _____

4. Pam catches the ball.   _____

5. Her team wins.   _____

6. The game ends.   _____

Level 2 Unit 2 **The Sentence** (Use with pupil book pages 43–44.)
Skill: Students will identify sentences.

LANGUAGE AND USAGE

5 | Telling Sentences

> ► A **telling sentence** tells something. It begins with a capital letter. It ends with a period.
>
> **M**y friends come for dinner**.**
> **E**veryone helps**.**

Write each correct telling sentence.

★ Dad cooks fish
Dad cooks fish.

Dad cooks fish.

1. Aunt Ida bakes apples.
aunt Ida bakes apples.

_____

_____

2. the kitchen smells good.
The kitchen smells good.

_____

_____

3. Abe sets the table.
Abe sets the table

_____

_____

Level 2 Unit 2   The Sentence   *(Use with pupil book pages 45–46.)*
Skill: Students will identify and will write statements, using capital letters and periods.

Name _____

LANGUAGE AND USAGE

6 | Questions

> ► A **question** asks something. It begins with a capital letter. It ends with a question mark.
>
> **W**hat things make you laugh**?**
> **D**o you laugh at a funny story**?**

Write the correct questions.

★ Do you tell jokes?
  do you tell jokes?

Do you tell jokes?

1. Do you smile at a surprise
   Do you smile at a surprise?

_____

- -

_____

2. What surprises do you like?
   what surprises do you like?

_____

- -

_____

3. do cartoons make you smile?
   Do cartoons make you smile?

_____

- -

_____

Level 2 Unit 2 The Sentence   *(Use with pupil book pages 47–48.)*
Skill: Students will identify and will write questions, using capital letters and question marks.

LANGUAGE AND USAGE

7 | Which Kind of Sentence?

> ▶ A **telling sentence** begins with a capital letter and ends with a period.
>
> **W**e visited a sheep farm**.**
>
> ▶ A **question** begins with a capital letter and ends with a question mark.
>
> **H**ave you been to a sheep farm**?**

Write **telling** after each telling sentence. Write **question** after each question.

★ Where do we get wool?   *question*

1. Wool comes from sheep.   _____

2. A sheep's wool grows thick.   _____

3. Do people cut the wool?   _____

4. Does that hurt the sheep?   _____

5. The sheep does not feel it.   _____

6. How do we use wool?   _____

Telling About One Idea

Every sentence in a story should tell about the one main idea.

   I helped my Dad make bread. We mixed flour and yeast and milk. We waited. ~~I wait for the bus.~~ We mixed the dough again. Then we baked the bread.

Cross out the picture that does not fit. Then cross out the sentence that does not fit.

We made clay. We mixed flour, salt, and oil in a large bowl. Grandma and I painted my bedroom blue. We used our hands to mix the clay. We added dry paint to the clay to turn it blue.

Telling Enough

When you write a story, be sure to tell enough.

Not Enough: Todd went out.
Enough: Todd went to the park.

Read this story. Do you think it tells enough?

Shelby and I went somewhere. Things were all over the sand. We heard noises. We got our feet wet.

Who is Shelby? Where did they go? What was on the sand? What noises did they hear? How did they get their feet wet? Add words to make the story tell enough.

_____

My _____ Shelby and I went to

_____

_____ .

_____ _____

_____ and _____ were

_____

all over the sand. We heard _____ .

_____

We got our feet wet _____

Step 3: Revise

Have I added enough details?

yes ☐

Look at the picture and read the story. What was wrong with Mrs. Cale? What did the children do? Revise the story so that it tells enough. Add three details. Write between the lines. Cross out the sentence that does not fit.

My neighbor, Mrs. Cale, was hurt.   She needed

help.   Sue and I did some jobs for her.   Mrs. Cale

was happy.   Helping her was fun.   She has a cat.

THE WRITING PROCESS: A STORY ABOUT ME

Step 4: Proofread

	yes
Did I begin each sentence with a capital letter?	☐
Did I use correct end marks?	☐
Did I spell each word correctly?	☐

have you heard funny noises ?

Proofreading Marks

∧ Add.

— Take out.

= Make a capital letter.

/ Make a small letter.

Proofread these sentences. There are two mistakes in each sentence. Use proofreading marks to correct the mistakes. Use a dictionary to check spellings. Then write the sentences correctly on another piece of paper.

★ I heard ~~funy~~ funny noises.

I heard funny noises.

1 Mom and i went to the attic

2. What do you think mad the noise.

3. two squirrel chattered at us.

LANGUAGE AND USAGE

1 | **Naming Words**

> ▶ A word that names a person is called a **noun**.
>
> My **mother** drives a school bus.

Write the noun that names a person in each row. Draw a picture of the noun in the box.

★ ask   boy   make

<u>boy</u>

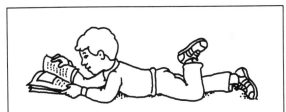

1. clown   in   tell

_____

2. happy   are   teacher

_____

3. baby   need   just

_____

4. doctor   funny   in

_____

Level 2　Unit 4　Nouns　　*(Use with pupil book pages 95–96.)*
Skill:　Students will identify nouns that name people.

LANGUAGE AND USAGE

2 | More Naming Words

> ▶ A noun names a person, a place, or a thing.
>
> person   thing   place
> The **teacher** hung my **picture** in the **hall**.

Write the noun that names a place or a thing in each sentence.

★ Our school is red.

                    school

1. Our room is sunny.

2. My desk is clean.

3. I sit next to the window.

4. The sun keeps me warm.

5. I can see my house.

6. I see the bus come.

LANGUAGE AND USAGE

3 | One and More Than One

▶ Add <u>s</u> to most nouns to name more than one.

one hill   two **hill<u>s</u>**
a river   many **river<u>s</u>**

Write the sentences. Use the nouns that name more than one.

★ The (riders, rider) go west.

The riders go west.

1. Their (horse, horses) are tired.

_____

- -

_____

2. The (wagon, wagons) bump along.

_____

- -

_____

3. The (days, day) are long and dusty.

_____

- -

_____

4. The (animal, animals) want to rest.

_____

- -

_____

LANGUAGE AND USAGE

4 | Adding <u>es</u>

> ► Add <u>es</u> to nouns that end with <u>x</u>, <u>ch</u>, <u>sh</u>, or <u>s</u> to name more than one.
>
> a dress   two **dresses**   a branch   some **branches**
> one fox   four **foxes**   one brush   many **brushes**

Write the noun that names more than one to finish each sentence.

★ Polly's and Gil's  **classes** went on a picnic.
(class, classes)

1. Their picnic was packed in _____ .
(box, boxes)

2. They sat on _____ .
(bench, benches)

3. Gil and Polly ate their _____ .
(lunches, lunch)

4. They used paper _____ .
(dishes, dish)

5. Gil poured milk into all the _____ .
(glass, glasses)

Level 2 Unit 4 Nouns   (Use with pupil book pages 101–102.)
Skill: Students will write plural nouns that end with *es*.

5 | Nouns That Change Spelling

> ► Some nouns change spelling to name more than one.
>
> | one man | many **men** |
> |---|---|
> | a woman | two **women** |
> | one child | six **children** |

Write the noun that names more than one in each
sentence.

★ Three __children__ are shopping.
(children, child)

1. Two _____ want red caps.
(child, children)

2. Four _____ are looking at ties.
(men, man)

3. Those two _____ need new shoes.
(woman, women)

4. Those _____ are buying belts.
(man, men)

5. Two _____ are trying on dresses.
(women, woman)

LANGUAGE AND USAGE

6 | Special Nouns

▶ Begin the names of special people, places, and things with capital letters.

Nouns	Special Nouns
girl	**A**licia
street	**B**irch **S**treet
town	**R**iverton
pet	**G**rover

The special nouns have lines drawn under them. Write the special nouns correctly.

★ Today <u>becky</u> goes to a new school.

Becky

1. She just moved to <u>lakeville</u>.

2. Her bus stops on <u>main street</u>.

3. Becky waves to her sister <u>mary</u>.

4. Her dog <u>rags</u> stays behind.

5. The driver named <u>fran</u> smiles.

LANGUAGE AND USAGE

7 | Words for Nouns

> ▶ A **pronoun** is a word that can take the place of a noun. <u>He</u>, <u>she</u>, <u>it</u>, and <u>they</u> are pronouns.
>
> | | |
> |---|---|
> | <u>Matt</u> called the cat. | **He** called the cat. |
> | <u>Jan</u> reached for the cat. | **She** reached for the cat. |
> | <u>The cat</u> was up a tree. | **It** was up a tree. |
> | <u>Matt and Jan</u> called for help. | **They** called for help. |

Write each sentence. Use the pronoun that can take the place of the underlined word or words.

★ <u>Our neighborhood</u> is very noisy. (It, They)

It is very noisy.

1. <u>Todd and Pam</u> have a pet duck. (She, They)

_____

_____

2. <u>The duck</u> quacks all day long. (It, They)

_____

_____

3. <u>Willie</u> wants a duck too. (It, He)

_____

_____

4. <u>Mom</u> says that one duck is enough. (She, He)

_____

_____

LANGUAGE AND USAGE

8 | Naming Yourself Last

▶ When you talk about another person and yourself, name yourself last.

Luke and I often work outside.

Write each sentence correctly.

★ (Jo and I, I and Jo) work hard.

Jo and I work hard.

1. Yesterday (I and Rosa, Rosa and I) cut the grass.

_____

_ _

_____

2. (I and Dan, Dan and I) will plant flowers.

_____

_ _

_____

3. (Rana and I, I and Rana) will wash windows.

_____

_ _

_____

4. On Friday (I and Rod, Rod and I) will rake.

_____

_ _

_____

5. On Saturday (Suki and I, I and Suki) will rest.

_____

_ _

_____

COMPOSITION SKILL: STORY

Parts of a Story

A story has a **beginning**, a **middle**, and an **end**.

Look at the pictures. They tell the beginning and end of a story. Draw a middle for the story in the box.

beginning

middle

end

Level 2   Unit 5   Story   *(Use with pupil book page 134.)*
Skill: Students will draw a middle for a story.

Step 3: Revise

	yes
Does my story have a beginning, a middle, and an end?	☐

The ending of this story is crossed out. Write a new ending for the story at the bottom of the page.

Tess and Abel were walking in the woods. They heard beautiful music. The children wanted to know where the music was coming from. Tess pointed to a small cave. The music was coming from inside. Abel and Tess looked into the cave. They saw a fox playing a small piano. ~~The children walked home for lunch~~.

_____

- -

_____

- -

_____

- -

_____

- -

_____

- -

_____

Step 4: Proofread

	yes
Did I begin and end each sentence correctly?	☐
Did I use verbs correctly?	☐
Did I spell each word correctly?	☐

waited   _bus_
s̲uji ~~wait~~ for the ~~buss~~.

Proofreading Marks

∧ Add.

— Take out.

≡ Make a capital letter.

/ Make a small letter.

Proofread these sentences. There are two mistakes in each sentence. Use proofreading marks to correct the mistakes. Use a dictionary to check spellings. Then write the sentences correctly on another piece of paper.

★ The bus ~~uas~~ _was_ /ate.

1. her friend Tim walk by.

2. He told her It was Saturday?

3. suji crossed the stret and went home.

LANGUAGE AND USAGE

1 | Action Words

> ▶ A **verb** names an action.
>
> A mother bear **stands** in the river.

Write the verb that finishes each sentence.

★ The bear __looks__ for fish.
(well, looks)

1. The baby bear _____ .
(watches, fox)

2. Fish _____ by the big bear.
(bell, swim)

3. The mother bear _____ .
(waits, holes)

4. Then she _____ fast.
(woods, moves)

5. The bear _____ up a big fish.
(holds, tree)

2 ▌Verbs That Tell About Now

> ▶ Add <u>s</u> to a verb that tells about one.
>
> One turtle **swims**.   Two turtles **swim**.

Write each sentence. Use the verb that tells about the
underlined naming part.

★ <u>Al and Li</u> (bring, brings) food.

Al and Li bring food.

1. <u>Li</u> (clean, cleans) the bowl.

_____

2. <u>Al and Li</u> (care, cares) for the turtles.

_____

3. <u>Li</u> (put, puts) the turtles in the tub.

_____

4. <u>The three turtles</u> (slide, slides).

_____

5. <u>Li</u> (place, places) them in the clean bowl.

_____

LANGUAGE AND USAGE

3 | Adding <u>ed</u>

▶ Add <u>ed</u> to a verb to show that something happened in the **past**.

Now I **play** a trick.   Yesterday I **play<u>ed</u>** a trick.

Write the verb that tells about the past to finish each sentence.

★ My brother and sister ____looked____ for me.
(look, looked)

1. I _____ behind my door.
(wait, waited)

2. I _____ very quiet.
(stayed, stay)

3. Cal and Beth _____ by my door.
(walked, walk)

4. I _____ out at them.
(jumped, jump)

5. We _____ at my trick.
(laugh, laughed)

Level 2   Unit 6   Verbs   *(Use with pupil book pages 155–156.)*
Skill: Students will write the past tense of regular verbs.

Name _____

4 | ran, run and came, come

▶ <u>Have</u> and <u>has</u> are **helping words**.
▶ Use helping words with <u>run</u> and <u>come</u>.
▶ Do not use helping words with <u>ran</u> and <u>came</u>.

Warm weather **came**.	The birds **have come** back.
A lamb **ran** past us.	It **has run** to the field.

Write the correct verb to finish each sentence.

★   Guy has (came, come) to my house.   <u>come</u>

1.   He (ran, run) here.   _____

2.   A deer (came, come) to my yard.   _____

3.   It (ran, run) away from us.   _____

4.   It has (came, come) back again.   _____

5.   We have (ran, run) quietly.   _____

6.   The deer (came, come) near us.   _____

Level 2   Unit 6   Verbs   *(Use with pupil book pages 157–158.)*
Skill: Students will use *ran, run, came,* and *come* correctly.

LANGUAGE AND USAGE

5 | saw, seen and went, gone

> ▶ Has and have are helping words.
> ▶ Use helping words with seen and gone.
> ▶ Do not use helping words with saw and went.
>
> We **went** to Mom's office.   I **have gone** there before.
> Julie **saw** the computers.   She **has seen** them before.

Write the correct verb to finish each sentence.

★ Julie and I (went, gone) to Dad's office.

Julie and I ___**went**___ to Dad's office.

1. Julie has (went, gone) to Dad's office before.

Julie has _____ to Dad's office before.

2. We (saw, seen) many tall tables.

We _____ many tall tables.

3. Julie has (saw, seen) Dad's drawing tools often.

Julie has _____ Dad's drawing tools often.

4. I (went, gone) home with a drawing.

I _____ home with a drawing.

LANGUAGE AND USAGE

6 | did, done and gave, given

> ▶ <u>Has</u> and <u>have</u> are helping words.
> ▶ Use helping words with <u>done</u> and <u>given</u>.
> ▶ Do not use helping words with <u>did</u> and <u>gave</u>.
>
> We **did** jobs.   We **have done** them before.
> Dad **gave** us directions.   He **has given** us his help.

Write the correct verb to finish each sentence.

★ Frank __did__ the breakfast dishes.
      (did, done)

1. I have _____ the dog her breakfast.
      (gave, given)

2. I _____ the baby her bath.
      (gave, given)

3. Mom has _____ us more jobs.
      (gave, given)

4. Frank and I have _____ a lot of work.
      (did, done)

5. Little Tim _____ nothing at all.
      (did, done)

LANGUAGE AND USAGE

7 | is and are

> ▸ Use <u>is</u> with one.
> ▸ Use <u>are</u> with more than one.
>
> This pool **is** long.   Many people **are** here.

Read each pair of sentences. Write the correct sentence.

★ Jim are in the pool. Jim is in the pool.

Jim is in the pool.

1. His crutches are here. His crutches is here.

_____

_____

2. Jim's parents is proud. Jim's parents are proud.

_____

_____

3. A smile is on Jim's face. A smile are on Jim's face.

_____

_____

4. Jim are a great swimmer. Jim is a great swimmer.

_____

_____

LANGUAGE AND USAGE

8 | was and were

> ▶ Use <u>was</u> with one.
> ▶ Use <u>were</u> with more than one.
>
> Emmy **was** in her seat.   Her friends **were** near her.

Read each pair of sentences. Write the correct sentence.

★ They was on a train. They were on a train.

They were on a train.

1. The seats were full. The seats was full.

   _____

   _____

2. The window was open. The window were open.

   _____

   _____

3. The friends were happy. The friends was happy.

   _____

   _____

4. The train were moving! The train was moving!

   _____

   _____

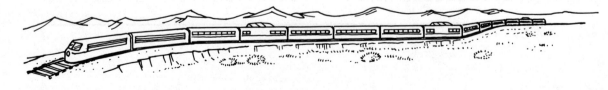

Houghton Mifflin English 2
Copyright © Houghton Mifflin Company. All rights reserved.

Level 2   Unit 6   Verbs   *(Use with pupil book pages 165–166.)*
Skill: Students will use *was* and *were* correctly.

LANGUAGE AND USAGE

9 ‖ Contractions

> ▶ A **contraction** is a short way of writing words.
> ▶ An **apostrophe** ' shows where letters have been left out.

do not	**don't**	is not	**isn't**
does not	**doesn't**	cannot	**can't**

Write each sentence. Use the contraction.

★ Kate (cannot, can't) find a shoe.

Kate can't find a shoe.

1. Her shoe (isn't, is not) in her closet.

_____

_____

2. It (cannot, can't) be in the washing machine.

_____

_____

3. Kate (does not, doesn't) know where to look now.

_____

_____

4. Shoes (do not, don't) walk by themselves.

_____

_____

What Is a Paragraph?

A **paragraph** is a group of sentences about one main idea. A paragraph is **indented.**

→ Painting is fun. Use different colors for a pretty picture. Show your picture to a friend.

Read each paragraph. Draw a line under the sentence that tells the main idea. Then write paragraph 2. The arrow shows you where to indent.

1.   You can make a peanut butter sandwich. Spread peanut butter on one piece of bread. Put another piece of bread on top. Eat it!

2.   Have a clean desk with your own litter bag. Tape a lunch bag to your desk. Throw your trash in it.

_____

→ _____

_____

_____

_____

_____

_____

Level 2   Unit 7   Instructions   *(Use with pupil book pages 199–200.)*
Skill: Students will identify the main idea of a paragraph and will write a paragraph correctly.

What Is a Topic Sentence?

A **topic sentence** tells the **main idea** of a paragraph.

Clay is easy to make. Mix flour, salt, and oil in a bowl. Add dry paint to make colored clay.

Read each paragraph. Draw a line under the topic sentence.

1. Cotton balls make a good snowman picture. Draw a snowman on a piece of paper. Draw two eyes, a nose, and a mouth with a marker. Add a hat. Glue cotton balls on your snowman. Your snowman is finished!

2. Make a birthday card for a friend. Fold your paper in half. Draw a picture on the front. Write a poem inside.

Step 3: Revise

	yes
Do I tell about one main idea?	☐
Do I have a topic sentence?	☐
Are there any steps I forgot?	☐
Are there any sentences that don't belong?	☐

Revise this paragraph. Cross out one sentence that does not belong. Add one step that has been forgotten. Write between the lines.

Washing my dog is hard work.   I love my dog.

First, I have to get him into the bathtub.   Then I

get him wet.   Next, I put soap on him.   Finally, I

dry him with a towel.

Step 4: Proofread

	yes
Did I begin and end each sentence correctly?	☐
Did I use verbs correctly?	☐
Did I spell each word correctly?	☐

circle
cut a ₿ig ~~cirkl?~~.
≡

Proofreading Marks

∧ Add.

— Take out.

≡ Make a capital letter.

/ Make a small letter.

Proofread these sentences. There are two mistakes in each sentence. Use proofreading marks to correct the mistakes. Use a dictionary to check spellings. Then write each sentence correctly on another piece of paper.

make
★ socks ~~mak~~ good puppets.
≡

_____
- -
_____

1. find an old white sock?

2. draw two, a nose, and a mouth on it.

3. Slip yor hand into the sock?

LANGUAGE AND USAGE

1 | How Something Looks

▶ **Adjectives** tell how something looks. They can tell size, shape, color, and how many.

Size: The airport was **huge**.
Shape: The runway was **long** and **flat**.
Color: A **blue** plane landed on the runway.
How Many: Mom drove **two** friends to the airport.

Write an adjective to finish each sentence.

★ <u>Three</u> airplanes were on the runway.
(Three, Jump)

1. A _____ pilot climbed into a jet.
(tall, ground)

2. _____ workers closed the doors.
(Two, Read)

3. The _____ jet took off.
(wings, silver)

4. A _____ plane was next.
(pencil, big)

Level 2 Unit 8 Adjectives *(Use with pupil book pages 219–220.)*
Skill: Students will write adjectives that describe size, shape, color, and how many.

2 | How Something Tastes and Smells

> ► Adjectives tell how something tastes and smells.
>
> **Taste:** Lois tastes the **fresh** fish.
> **Smell:** There is a **sweet** smell in the kitchen.

Draw a line under each adjective that tells how something tastes or smells. Then write the sentences.

★ Li's fish tastes (slow, <u>salty</u>).

Li's fish tastes salty.

1. She adds a taste of (soft, sour) lemon.

   _____

   _____

2. Lois likes the potatoes' (peppery, green) taste.

   _____

   _____

3. Li and Lois smell something (tall, fruity).

   _____

   _____

4. They smell (spicy, round) baked apples.

   _____

   _____

LANGUAGE AND USAGE

3 | **How Something Sounds and Feels**

> ► Adjectives tell how something sounds and feels.
>
> **Sound:** Those trucks are making a **honking** noise.
> **Feel:** They are driving on a **smooth** road.

Write the adjectives that tell how something sounds or feels.

★ Our road was very  .

(pink, bumpy)

1. Cars made _____ noises on it.

(loud, cold)

2. People worked in the _____ sun.

(big, hot)

3. Tools made _____ sounds.

(many, clicking)

4. The _____ machines came close to our house.

(noisy, new)

5. The tar felt _____ under my feet.

(blue, sticky)

LANGUAGE AND USAGE

4 | Adding <u>er</u> and <u>est</u>

> ▶ Add <u>er</u> to compare two people or things.
> ▶ Add <u>est</u> to compare more than two people or things.

tall   tall**er**   tall**est**

Write the correct word for each sentence.

★ The woods are ___quieter___ than the street.

(quieter, quietest)

1. The woods are the _____ of all places.

(quieter, quietest)

2. This tree is _____ than that one.

(older, oldest)

3. That tree is the _____ of all the trees.

(older, oldest)

4. It is the _____ of these three trees.

(taller, tallest)

COMPOSITION SKILL: DESCRIPTION

Using Exact Words

Use **exact** words to describe something clearly.

A truck <u>has</u> a car.
A truck **pulls** a car.

Write each sentence, using the exact word.

1. Look at that old (thing, car).

_____

- -

_____

2. The front (part, window) is broken.

_____

- -

_____

3. (Two, Some) of the tires are flat.

_____

- -

_____

4. The (stuff, paint) is peeling all over.

_____

- -

_____

Level 2   Unit 9   Description   (Use with pupil book page 248.)
Skill: Students will use exact words in sentences.

Step 3: Revise

	yes
Have I used exact words?	☐
Have I used details that tell how something looks, sounds, tastes, smells, or feels?	☐

Revise this paragraph. Write an exact word in place of each underlined word. Add a detail to tell how the night looked, sounded, smelled, or felt. Write between the lines.

It was a beautiful night. The wind felt <u>nice</u>.

The moon was <u>big</u>. <u>Lots</u> of <u>things</u> were shining.

A shooting star <u>went</u> across the dark sky. I heard

noises. The air smelled <u>good</u>.

THE WRITING PROCESS: DESCRIPTION

Step 4: Proofread

	yes
Did I begin and end each sentence correctly?	☐
Did I spell each word correctly?	☐

brother
My ~~brothr~~ is a ₵ircus clown~~?~~.

Proofreading Marks

∧	Add.
—	Take out.
≡	Make a capital letter.
/	Make a small letter.

Proofread these sentences. There are two mistakes in each sentence. Use proofreading marks to correct the mistakes. Use a dictionary to check spellings. Then write each sentence correctly on another piece of paper.

★ he ~~hes~~ a silly costume.
   ≡   has

He has a silly costume.

1. His fas is painted White.

2. his funny nose is soft and round?

3. His hair is pink and blew

MECHANICS

1 | Days

> ▶ Use capital letters to begin the names of the days of the week.
>
> **S**unday   **T**uesday   **T**hursday   **S**aturday
> **M**onday   **W**ednesday   **F**riday
>
> Ned will take his piano lesson on **T**uesday.

Draw a line under the correct word. Then write the sentence correctly.

★ Ned cleans on (friday, <u>Friday</u>).

Ned cleans on Friday.

1. Ned visits Gramps on (Sunday, sunday).

_____

2. On (thursday, Thursday) Ned plays soccer.

_____

3. Ned studies on (Monday, monday).

_____

4. Ned has a picnic on (Saturday, saturday).

_____

MECHANICS

2 | Holidays

▶ Begin the names of holidays with capital letters.

Today is **F**ather's **D**ay.

Write the names of the underlined holidays correctly.

★ Does school begin before <u>labor day</u>?

Labor Day

1. We have a picnic on <u>flag day</u>.

   _____

   -

   _____

2. Do you go to school on <u>columbus day</u>?

   _____

   -

   _____

3. Grandma will be here on <u>thanksgiving day</u>.

   _____

   -

   _____

4. I gave Dad a card for <u>valentine's day</u>.

   _____

   -

   _____

5. On <u>presidents' day</u> we saw a parade.

   _____

   -

   _____

3 | Months

> ▶ Begin the names of the months with capital letters.

January	**M**ay	**S**eptember
February	**J**une	**O**ctober
March	**J**uly	**N**ovember
April	**A**ugust	**D**ecember

In **J**anuary Mom ordered seeds for our garden.

Write the names of the underlined months correctly.

★ In <u>march</u> we planted peas.

March

1. It rained for nine days in <u>april</u>.

2. In <u>may</u> Dad planted corn.

3. In <u>june</u> we picked peas.

4. I weeded the garden in <u>july</u>.

5. In <u>august</u> we watered the garden.

6. In <u>september</u> we ate a lot of corn.

MECHANICS

4 | **Titles for People**

> ► A title begins with a capital letter.
> ► Put a period after <u>Mrs.</u>, <u>Mr.</u>, <u>Ms.</u>, and <u>Dr.</u>
>   The title <u>Miss</u> does not have a period.
>
> **Mrs.** Perez   **Mr.** Rutter   **Ms.** Chung
>   **Dr.** Finlay   **Miss** Lee

Write the titles and names correctly.

★ ms Hanks

Ms. Hanks

1. dr Fisher

2. miss Allen

3. mr Kan

4. mrs. Dow

5. Mr Nelson

6. dr Ramos

7. ms. Rosen

MECHANICS

5 | **Writing Book Titles**

▶ Begin the first word, the last word, and each important word in a book title with a capital letter. Draw a line under the title.

My favorite book is **M**ake **W**ay for **D**ucklings.

Write the correct book titles.

★ King of the cats   King of the Cats

King of the Cats

1. One Morning in Maine   one morning in Maine

   _____

2. Whistle for Willie   Whistle for Willie

   _____

3. Green Eggs and ham   Green Eggs and Ham

   _____

4. William's Doll   William's Doll

   _____

MECHANICS

6 | Ending Sentences

> ▶ A telling sentence ends with a period.
>
> Those blue flowers are pretty**.**
>
> ▶ A question ends with a question mark.
>
> Did someone plant them there**?**

Write the correct end mark for each sentence. Write **Q**
after each question. Write **T** after each telling sentence.

★ How do flowers make new plants ___**?**___   ___Q___

1. Some flowers make seeds _____   _____

2. Do the seeds fall to the ground _____   _____

3. Rain and sun make the seeds grow _____   _____

4. Do birds carry flower seeds _____   _____

5. Birds drop the seeds in new places _____   _____

6. Do other animals carry seeds _____   _____

MECHANICS

7 ▍ Commas in Dates

> ▶ A **date** tells a month, a day, and a year.
> ▶ Use a **comma ,** between the day and the year in a date.
>
> Eva was born February 2, 1982.

Write the correct date.

★ March 7, 1990   March 7 1990

March 7, 1990

1. September, 18 1955   September 18, 1955

_____

- - - - - - - - - - - - - - - - - - - -

_____

2. July 12, 1979   July 12 1979

_____

- - - - - - - - - - - - - - - - - - - -

_____

3. August 4, 1985   August, 4 1985

_____

- - - - - - - - - - - - - - - - - - - -

_____

4. June 28 1983   June 28, 1983

_____

- - - - - - - - - - - - - - - - - - - -

_____

MECHANICS

8 | **Commas with Names of Places**

> ▶ Use a comma between the name of a city and the name of a state.
>
> Daniel goes to camp in Camden, Maine.

Write each underlined city and state correctly. Put a comma in the correct place.

★ Daniel lives in <u>Detroit Michigan</u>.

Detroit, Michigan

1. Joey comes to camp from <u>Omaha Nebraska</u>.

_____

- - - - - - - - - - - - - - - - - - - -

_____

2. Joey travels through <u>Chicago Illinois</u>.

_____

- - - - - - - - - - - - - - - - - - - -

_____

3. Mary comes from <u>Richmond Virginia</u>.

_____

- - - - - - - - - - - - - - - - - - - -

_____

4. Mary rides on a train from <u>Baltimore Maryland</u>.

_____

- - - - - - - - - - - - - - - - - - - -

_____

COMPOSITION SKILL: LETTERS

Kinds of Letters

> Some letters say thank you. Some letters tell someone to get well. Invitations ask someone to come to something.

Read the letter below. Then answer the questions.

October 19, 1990

Dear Nita,

Can you come to my birthday party on Saturday? Come to the ice-skating rink at noon.

Your friend,
Mara

1. What kind of letter is this?

2. Who will receive the letter?

3. Who wrote the letter?

4. On what day is the party?

5. What time is the party?

Parts of a Letter

Every letter has five parts. The parts are the **date**, the **greeting**, the **body**, the **closing**, and the **name**.

Read this letter. Then write the answers to the questions.

April 25, 1990

Dear Marty,

Our new house is fun. There is a big apple tree in the yard. Can you come for a visit next weekend? We could build a great tree house!

Your friend,
Jessie

1. What is the date? _____

2. What is the greeting? _____

3. What is the closing? _____

4. Who wrote the letter? _____

5. Who will receive the letter? _____

Step 3: Revise

	yes
Does my letter tell enough?	☐
Does my letter have all five parts?	☐

Revise Jean's letter. Add two details to make her letter more interesting. Add the missing part to the letter. Write between the lines.

September 19, 1990

Dear Penny,

I liked seeing you on Saturday. It was good to

meet your friends. I really liked playing with you. I

hope that we can see each other again soon.

Jean

Step 4: Proofread

	yes	Proofreading Marks
Did I use capital letters correctly?	☐	∧ Add.
Did I spell each word correctly?	☐	— Take out.
		= Make a capital letter.
		/ Make a small letter.

mail
<u>i</u> got a present in the ~~mal~~ today.

Proofread this letter. There are six mistakes. Use proofreading marks to correct the mistakes. Use a dictionary to check spellings. Then write the letter correctly on another piece of paper.

March 16 1990

Dear Aunt May,

thank yow for the scarf. I love the bright colers? I wore it

today. I hope that you can come to stae with us soon.

Love,

Kristy

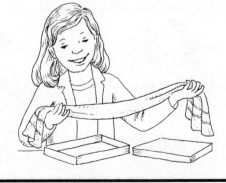

Teacher's Annotated Pages

Worksheet 2

Name _____

2 | Naming Part

▶ The **naming part** of a sentence tells whom or what a sentence is about.

The children bring pets to school.
Their show begins at noon.

Write the naming part to finish each sentence.

★ **Ted** drops his frog, Bully.
(Smiled, Ted)

1. **Bully** hops onto Mr. Pratt's head.
(Bully, Moves)

2. **Mr. Pratt** jumps in surprise.
(Sits down, Mr. Pratt)

3. **His hat** falls into the box.
(Blows away, His hat)

4. **The teacher** covers the box.
(The teacher, Stands)

5. **The frog** wins a prize.
(The frog, Swims away)

Worksheet 1

Name _____

1 | What Is a Sentence?

▶ A **sentence** tells what someone or something does.

Grandma plants her garden.
The flowers bloom.

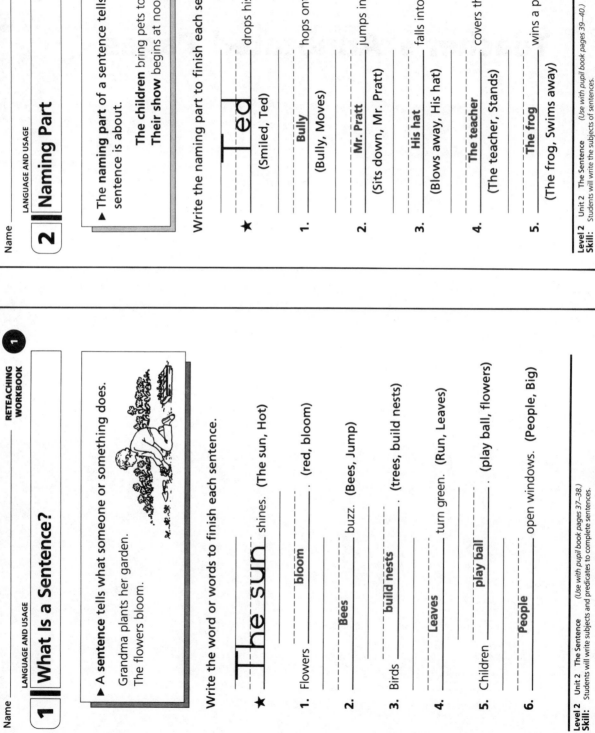

Write the word or words to finish each sentence.

★ **The sun** shines. (The sun, Hot)

1. Flowers **bloom** . (red, bloom)

2. **Bees** buzz. (Bees, Jump)

3. Birds **build nests** . (trees, build nests)

4. **Leaves** turn green. (Run, Leaves)

5. Children **play ball** . (play ball, flowers)

6. **People** open windows. (People, Big)

Level 2   Unit 2   The Sentence   (Use with pupil book pages 37–38.)
Skill: Students will write subjects and predicates to complete sentences.

T1

Name _____

LANGUAGE AND USAGE

4 | Is It a Sentence?

▶ A sentence has a naming part and an action part.

naming part   +   action part
The baseball game   **begins.**

The baseball game begins.

Write **yes** beside each group of words that is a sentence.
Write **no** beside each group of words that is not a sentence.

★ Rico bats.   _yes_

1. the players   _no_

2. The ball flies high.   _yes_

3. keeps running   _no_

4. Pam catches the ball.   _yes_

5. Her team wins.   _yes_

6. The game ends.   _yes_

Level 2   Unit 2   The Sentence   (Use with pupil book pages 43–44.)
Skill: Students will identify sentences.

Name _____

LANGUAGE AND USAGE

3 | Action Part

▶ The **action part** of a sentence tells what is happening.

The team **runs every day.**
I **watch the track meet.**

Write the action part to finish each sentence.

★ The games _start at noon_ .
(in the morning, start at noon)

1. Rosa _runs short races_ .
(on the track, runs short races)

2. Paul _jumps_ .
(up and over again, jumps)

3. Ann _runs long races_ .
(runs long races, very short jumps)

4. Carlos _throws a ball_ .
(throws a ball, heavy and round)

5. I _cheer for them_ .
(my fast friends, cheer for them)

Level 2   Unit 2   The Sentence   (Use with pupil book pages 41–42.)
Skill: Students will write the predicates of sentences.

6 | Questions

▶ **A question** asks something. It begins with a capital letter. It ends with a question mark.

What things make you laugh**?**
Do you laugh at a funny story**?**

Write the correct questions.

★ Do you tell jokes?
do you tell jokes?

Do you tell jokes?

1. Do you smile at a surprise
   Do you smile at a surprise?

   Do you smile at a surprise?

2. What surprises do you like?
   what surprises do you like?

   What surprises do you like?

3. do cartoons make you smile?
   Do cartoons make you smile?

   Do cartoons make you smile?

---

5 | Telling Sentences

▶ **A telling sentence** tells something. It begins with a capital letter. It ends with a period.

My friends come for dinner.
Everyone helps.

Write each correct telling sentence.

★ Dad cooks fish
Dad cooks fish.

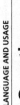

Dad cooks fish.

1. Aunt Ida bakes apples.
   aunt Ida bakes apples.

   Aunt Ida bakes apples.

2. the kitchen smells good.
   The kitchen smells good.

   The kitchen smells good.

3. Abe sets the table.
   Abe sets the table

   Abe sets the table.

Name _____

Telling About One Idea

Every sentence in a story should tell about the one main idea.

I helped my Dad make bread. We mixed flour and yeast and milk. ~~We waited. I wait for the bus.~~ We mixed the dough again. Then we baked the bread.

Cross out the picture that does not fit. Then cross out the sentence that does not fit.

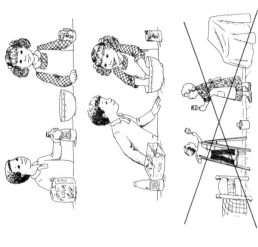

We made clay. We mixed flour, salt, and oil in a large bowl. ~~Grandma and I painted my bedroom blue.~~ We used our hands to mix the clay. We added dry paint to the clay to turn it blue.

Level 2   Unit 3   A Story About Me   (Use with pupil book pages 76–77.)
Skill: Students will identify a picture and a sentence that do not keep to the main idea.

Name _____

7 │ Which Kind of Sentence?

▶ A **telling sentence** begins with a capital letter and ends with a period.

   We visited a sheep farm.

▶ A **question** begins with a capital letter and ends with a question mark.

   Have you been to a sheep farm?

Write **telling** after each telling sentence. Write **question** after each question.

★ Where do we get wool?   ___question___

1. Wool comes from sheep.   _____telling_____

2. A sheep's wool grows thick.   _____telling_____

3. Do people cut the wool?   _____question_____

4. Does that hurt the sheep?   _____question_____

5. The sheep does not feel it.   _____telling_____

6. How do we use wool?   _____question_____

Level 2   Unit 2   The Sentence   (Use with pupil book pages 49–50.)
Skill: Students will distinguish between statements and questions.

Step 3: Revise

Have I added enough details?

yes ☐

Look at the picture and read the story. What was wrong with Mrs. Cale? What did the children do? Revise the story so that it tells enough. Add three details. Write between the lines. Cross out the sentence that does not fit. Sample answers:

She had a broken leg.

My neighbor, Mrs. Cale, was hurt.∧ She needed

I washed the dishes. Sue cleaned the floor.

help. Sue and I did some jobs for her.∧ Mrs. Cale

was happy. Helping her was fun. ~~She has a cat.~~

Level 2 Unit 3 A Story About Me (Use with pupil book pages 86–87.)
Skill: Students will revise a story, adding details.

Telling Enough

When you write a story, be sure to tell enough.

Not Enough: Todd went out.
Enough: Todd went to the park.

Read this story. Do you think it tells enough?

Shelby and I went somewhere. Things were all over the sand. We heard noises. We got our feet wet.

Who is Shelby? Where did they go? What was on the sand? What noises did they hear? How did they get their feet wet? Add words to make the story tell enough.

_____ Answers will vary. _____ Shelby and I went to

My _____

_____ and _____ were

all over the sand. We heard _____ .

We got our feet wet _____ .

Level 2 Unit 3 A Story About Me (Use with pupil book pages 78–79.)
Skill: Students will generate story details.

Name _____

1 | Naming Words

▶ A word that names a person is called a **noun**.

My **mother** drives a school bus.

Write the noun that names a person in each row. Draw a picture of the noun in the box.

★ ask   boy   make

boy

1. clown   in   tell

clown

2. happy   are   teacher

teacher

3. baby   need   just

baby

4. doctor   funny   in

doctor

Level 2   Unit 4   Nouns   (Use with pupil book pages 95–96.)
Skill: Students will identify nouns that name people.

Name _____

Step 4: Proofread

	yes
Did I begin each sentence with a capital letter?	☐
Did I use correct end marks?	☐
Did I spell each word correctly?	☐

Proofreading Marks

∧ Add.
— Take out.
≡ Make a capital letter.
/ Make a small letter.

have you heard funny noises?

Proofread these sentences. There are two mistakes in each sentence. Use proofreading marks to correct the mistakes. Use a dictionary to check spellings. Then write the sentences correctly on another piece of paper.

★ I heard funny noises.

I heard funny noises.

1. Mom and i went to the attic.

2. What do you think made the noise.?

3. two squirrels chattered at us.

Level 2   Unit 3   A Story About Me   (Use with pupil book pages 88–89.)
Skill: Students will proofread sentences.

T6

3 | One and More Than One

▶ Add s to most nouns to name more than one.

person		
one hill	two **hills**	
a river	many **rivers**	

Write the sentences. Use the nouns that name more than one.

★ The (riders, rider) go west.

The riders go west.

1. Their (horse, horses) are tired.

   Their horses are tired.

2. The (wagon, wagons) bump along.

   The wagons bump along.

3. The (days, day) are long and dusty.

   The days are long and dusty.

4. The (animal, animals) want to rest.

   The animals want to rest.

---

2 | More Naming Words

▶ A noun names a person, a place, or a thing.

| person | thing | place |
| The **teacher** hung my **picture** in the **hall**. | | |

Write the noun that names a place or a thing in each sentence.

★ Our school is red.

school

1. Our room is sunny.

   room

2. My desk is clean.

   desk

3. I sit next to the window.

   window

4. The sun keeps me warm.

   sun

5. I can see my house.

   house

6. I see the bus come.

   bus

Name _____

5 | Nouns That Change Spelling

▶ Some nouns change spelling to name more than one.

one man	many **men**
a woman	two **women**
one child	six **children**

Write the noun that names more than one in each sentence.

★ Three **children** are shopping.
(children, child)

1. Two **children** want red caps.
(child, children)

2. Four **men** are looking at ties.
(men, man)

3. Those two **women** need new shoes.
(woman, women)

4. Those **men** are buying belts.
(man, men)

5. Two **women** are trying on dresses.
(women, woman)

Level 2   Unit 4   Nouns   (Use with pupil book pages 103–104.)
Skill: Students will write nouns that change their spelling in the plural form.

Name _____

4 | Adding es

▶ Add es to nouns that end with x, ch, sh, or s to name more than one.

| a dress | two **dresses** | a branch | some **branches** |
| one fox | four **foxes** | one brush | many **brushes** |

Write the noun that names more than one to finish each sentence.

★ Polly's and Gil's **classes** went on a picnic.
(class, classes)

1. Their picnic was packed in **boxes** .
(box, boxes)

2. They sat on **benches** .
(bench, benches)

3. Gil and Polly ate their **lunches** .
(lunches, lunch)

4. They used paper **dishes** .
(dishes, dish)

5. Gil poured milk into all the **glasses** .
(glass, glasses)

Level 2   Unit 4   Nouns   (Use with pupil book pages 101–102.)
Skill: Students will write plural nouns that end with es.

7 | Words for Nouns

▶ **A pronoun** is a word that can take the place of a noun. He, she, it, and they are pronouns.

Matt called the cat.	**He** called the cat.
Jan reached for the cat.	**She** reached for the cat.
The cat was up a tree.	**It** was up a tree.
Matt and Jan called for help.	**They** called for help.

Write each sentence. Use the pronoun that can take the place of the underlined word or words. (It, They)

★ Our neighborhood is very noisy. (It, They)

It is very noisy.

1. Todd and Pam have a pet duck. (She, They)

They have a pet duck.

2. The duck quacks all day long. (It, They)

It quacks all day long.

3. Willie wants a duck too. (It, He)

He wants a duck too.

4. Mom says that one duck is enough. (She, He)

She says that one duck is enough.

---

6 | Special Nouns

▶ Begin the names of special people, places, and things with capital letters.

Nouns	Special Nouns
girl	**A**licia
street	**B**irch **S**treet
town	**R**iverton
pet	**G**rover

The special nouns have lines drawn under them. Write the special nouns correctly.

★ Today becky goes to a new school.

Becky

1. She just moved to lakeville.

Lakeville

2. Her bus stops on main street.

Main Street

3. Becky waves to her sister mary.

Mary

4. Her dog rags stays behind.

Rags

5. The driver named fran smiles.

Fran

Name _____

COMPOSITION SKILL: STORY

Parts of a Story

A story has a **beginning**, a **middle**, and an **end**.

Look at the pictures. They tell the beginning and end of a story. Draw a middle for the story in the box.
Answers will vary.

beginning

middle

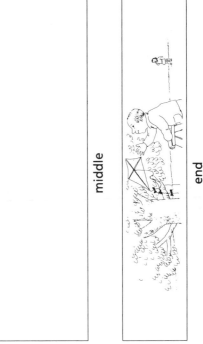

end

Level 2   Unit 5   Story   *(Use with pupil book page 134.)*
Skill: Students will draw a middle for a story.

Name _____

LANGUAGE AND USAGE

8 | Naming Yourself Last

▶ When you talk about another person and yourself, name yourself last.

    Luke and I often work outside.

Write each sentence correctly.

★ (Jo and I, I and Jo) work hard.

Jo and I work hard.

1. Yesterday (I and Rosa, Rosa and I) cut the grass.

   Yesterday Rosa and I cut the grass.

2. (I and Dan, Dan and I) will plant flowers.

   Dan and I will plant flowers.

3. (Rana and I, I and Rana) will wash windows.

   Rana and I will wash windows.

4. On Friday (I and Rod, Rod and I) will rake.

   On Friday Rod and I will rake.

5. On Saturday (Suki and I, I and Suki) will rest.

   On Saturday Suki and I will rest.

Level 2   Unit 4   Nouns   *(Use with pupil book pages 109–110.)*
Skill: Students will use *I* correctly.

Step 4: Proofread

	yes
Did I begin and end each sentence correctly?	☐
Did I use verbs correctly?	☐
Did I spell each word correctly?	☐

waited   bus
Suji ~~wait~~ for the ~~buss~~.

Proofreading Marks

∧ Add.
— Take out.
≡ Make a capital letter.
/ Make a small letter.

Proofread these sentences. There are two mistakes in each sentence. Use proofreading marks to correct the mistakes. Use a dictionary to check spellings. Then write the sentences correctly on another piece of paper.

★ The bus ~~was~~ /late.
                was

The bus was late.

1. her friend Tim ~~walk~~ by.
              walked

2. He told her/It was Saturday?

3. Suji crossed the ~~stret~~ and went home.
                    street

Step 3: Revise

	yes
Does my story have a beginning, a middle, and an end?	☐

The ending of this story is crossed out. Write a new ending for the story at the bottom of the page.

Tess and Abel were walking in the woods. They heard beautiful music. The children wanted to know where the music was coming from. Tess pointed to a small cave. The music was coming from inside. Abel and Tess looked into the cave. They saw a fox playing a small piano. ~~The children walked home for lunch.~~

Answers will vary.

Page 25

Name _____

LANGUAGE AND USAGE

1 | Action Words

▶ **A verb** names an action.

A mother bear **stands** in the river.

Write the verb that finishes each sentence.

★ The bear **looks** for fish.
(well, looks)

1. The baby bear **watches** _____ .
(watches, fox)

2. Fish **swim** _____ by the big bear.
(bell, swim)

3. The mother bear **waits** _____ .
(waits, holes)

4. Then she **moves** _____ fast.
(woods, moves)

5. The bear **holds** _____ up a big fish.
(holds, tree)

Level 2   Unit 6   Verbs   *(Use with pupil book pages 151–152.)*
Skill: Students will write verbs to complete sentences.

Page 26

Name _____

LANGUAGE AND USAGE

2 | Verbs That Tell About Now

▶ Add **s** to a verb that tells about one.

One turtle **swims**.   Two turtles **swim**.

Write each sentence. Use the verb that tells about the underlined naming part.

★ Al and Li (bring, brings) food.

Al and Li bring food.

1. Li (clean, cleans) the bowl.

Li cleans the bowl.

2. Al and Li (care, cares) for the turtles.

Al and Li care for the turtles.

3. Li (put, puts) the turtles in the tub.

Li puts the turtles in the tub.

4. The three turtles (slide, slides).

The three turtles slide.

5. Li (place, places) them in the clean bowl.

Li places them in the clean bowl.

Level 2   Unit 6   Verbs   *(Use with pupil book pages 153–154.)*
Skill: Students will choose present tense verbs that agree with their subjects.

4 | ran, run and came, come

▶ Have and has are **helping words**.
▶ Use helping words with run and come.
▶ Do not use helping words with ran and came.

Warm weather **came**.   The birds **have come** back.
A lamb **ran** past us.   It **has run** to the field.

Write the correct verb to finish each sentence.

★ Guy has (came, come) to my house.   **come**

1. He (ran, run) here.   **ran**

2. A deer (came, come) to my yard.   **came**

3. It (ran, run) away from us.   **ran**

4. It has (came, come) back again.   **come**

5. We have (ran, run) quietly.   **run**

6. The deer (came, come) near us.   **came**

---

3 | Adding ed

▶ Add ed to a verb to show that something happened in
the **past**.

Now I **play** a trick.   Yesterday I **played** a trick.

Write the verb that tells about the past to finish each
sentence.

★ My brother and sister ___ **looked** ___ for me.
(look, looked)

1. I ___ **waited** ___ behind my door.
(wait, waited)

2. I ___ **stayed** ___ very quiet.
(stayed, stay)

3. Cal and Beth ___ **walked** ___ by my door.
(walked, walk)

4. I ___ **jumped** ___ out at them.
(jumped, jump)

5. We ___ **laughed** ___ at my trick.
(laugh, laughed)

Level 2   Unit 6   Verbs   *(Use with pupil book pages 155–156.)*
Skill: Students will write the past tense of regular verbs.

T13

Name _____

6 | did, done and gave, given

▲ Has and have are helping words.
▲ Use helping words with done and given.
▲ Do not use helping words with did and gave.

We **did** jobs.   We **have done** them before.
Dad **gave** us directions.   He **has given** us his help.

Write the correct verb to finish each sentence.

★ Frank _____**did**_____ the breakfast dishes.
(did, done)

1. I have _____**given**_____ the dog her breakfast.
(gave, given)

2. I _____**gave**_____ the baby her bath.
(gave, given)

3. Mom has _____**given**_____ us more jobs.
(gave, given)

4. Frank and I have _____**done**_____ a lot of work.
(did, done)

5. Little Tim _____**did**_____ nothing at all.
(did, done)

Level 2   Unit 6   Verbs   (Use with pupil book pages 161–162.)
Skill: Students will use did, done, gave, and given correctly.

Name _____

5 | saw, seen and went, gone

▲ Has and have are helping words.
▲ Use helping words with seen and gone.
▲ Do not use helping words with saw and went.

We **went** to Mom's office.   I **have gone** there before.
Julie **saw** the computers.   She **has seen** them before.

Write the correct verb to finish each sentence.

★ Julie and I (went, gone) to Dad's office.

Julie and I _____**went**_____ to Dad's office.

1. Julie has (went, gone) to Dad's office before.

Julie has _____**gone**_____ to Dad's office before.

2. We (saw, seen) many tall tables.

We _____**saw**_____ many tall tables.

3. Julie has (saw, seen) Dad's drawing tools often.

Julie has _____**seen**_____ Dad's drawing tools often.

4. I (went, gone) home with a drawing.

_____**went**_____ home with a drawing.

Level 2   Unit 6   Verbs   (Use with pupil book pages 159–160.)
Skill: Students will use saw, seen, went, and gone correctly.

LANGUAGE AND USAGE

8 | was and were

▶ Use **was** with one.
▶ Use **were** with more than one.

Emmy **was** in her seat.   Her friends **were** near her.

Read each pair of sentences. Write the correct sentence.

★ They was on a train. They were on a train.

They were on a train.

1. The seats were full. The seats was full.

   The seats were full.

2. The window was open. The window were open.

   The window was open.

3. The friends were happy. The friends was happy.

   The friends were happy.

4. The train were moving! The train was moving!

   The train was moving!

LANGUAGE AND USAGE

7 | is and are

▶ Use **is** with one.
▶ Use **are** with more than one.

This pool **is** long.   Many people **are** here.

Read each pair of sentences. Write the correct sentence.

★ Jim are in the pool. Jim is in the pool.

Jim is in the pool.

1. His crutches are here. His crutches is here.

   His crutches are here.

2. Jim's parents is proud. Jim's parents are proud.

   Jim's parents are proud.

3. A smile is on Jim's face. A smile are on Jim's face.

   A smile is on Jim's face.

4. Jim are a great swimmer. Jim is a great swimmer.

   Jim is a great swimmer.

T15

Name _____

What Is a Paragraph?

A paragraph is a group of sentences about one main idea. A paragraph is **indented**.

➤ Painting is fun. Use different colors for a pretty picture. Show your picture to a friend.

Read each paragraph. Draw a line under the sentence that tells the main idea. Then write paragraph 2. The arrow shows you where to indent.

1. You can make a peanut butter sandwich. Spread peanut butter on one piece of bread. Put another piece of bread on top. Eat it!

2. Have a clean desk with your own litter bag. Tape a lunch bag to your desk. Throw your trash in it.

_____

➤ Have a clean desk with your own litter bag. Tape a

_____

lunch bag to your desk. Throw your trash in it.

_____

Level 2 Unit 7 Instructions (Use with pupil book pages 199–200.)
Skill: Students will identify the main idea of a paragraph and will write a paragraph correctly.

Name _____

9 Contractions

▲ **A contraction** is a short way of writing words.
▲ An **apostrophe** ' shows where letters have been left out.

do not	**don't**
does not	**doesn't**
is not	**isn't**
cannot	**can't**

Write each sentence. Use the contraction.

★ Kate (cannot, can't) find a shoe.

Kate can't find a shoe.

1. Her shoe (isn't, is not) in her closet.

Her shoe isn't in her closet.

2. It (cannot, can't) be in the washing machine.

It can't be in the washing machine.

3. Kate (does not, doesn't) know where to look now.

Kate doesn't know where to look now.

4. Shoes (do not, don't) walk by themselves.

Shoes don't walk by themselves.

Level 2 Unit 6 Verbs (Use with pupil book pages 167–168.)
Skill: Students will identify contractions.

Step 3: Revise

Do I tell about one main idea?

Do I have a topic sentence?

Are there any steps I forgot?

Are there any sentences that don't belong?

yes ☐ ☐ ☐ ☐

Revise this paragraph. Cross out one sentence that does not belong. Add one step that has been forgotten. Write between the lines.

Washing my dog is hard work. ~~I love my dog.~~

First, I have to get him into the bathtub.   Then I

get him wet.   Next, I put soap on him. **Then I rinse him off.** Finally, I
∧

dry him with a towel.

What Is a Topic Sentence?

A **topic sentence** tells the **main idea** of a paragraph.

Clay is easy to make. Mix flour, salt, and oil in a bowl. Add dry paint to make colored clay.

Read each paragraph. Draw a line under the topic sentence.

1. Cotton balls make a good snowman picture. Draw a snowman on a piece of paper. Draw two eyes, a nose, and a mouth with a marker. Add a hat. Glue cotton balls on your snowman. Your snowman is finished!

2. Make a birthday card for a friend. Fold your paper in half. Draw a picture on the front. Write a poem inside.

Name _____

1 | How Something Looks

▶ **Adjectives** tell how something looks. They can tell size, shape, color, and how many.

Size: The airport was **huge**.
Shape: The runway was **long** and **flat**.
Color: A **blue** plane landed on the runway.
How Many: Mom drove **two** friends to the airport.

Write an adjective to finish each sentence.

★ **Three** airplanes were on the runway.
(Three, Jump)

1. A **tall** pilot climbed into a jet.
(tall, ground)

2. **Two** workers closed the doors.
(Two, Read)

3. The **silver** jet took off.
(wings, silver)

4. A **big** plane was next.
(pencil, big)

Name _____

Step 4: Proofread

	yes
Did I begin and end each sentence correctly?	☐
Did I use verbs correctly?	☐
Did I spell each word correctly?	☐

Proofreading Marks

∧ Add.
— Take out.
≡ Make a capital letter.
/ Make a small letter.

cut a *B*ig *circle* *~~cirkl~~*?.

Proofread these sentences. There are two mistakes in each sentence. Use proofreading marks to correct the mistakes. Use a dictionary to check spellings. Then write each sentence correctly on another piece of paper.

★ *make*
socks ~~mak~~ good puppets.
≡

Socks make good puppets.

1. find an old white sock?.
   ≡

2. draw two, a nose, and a mouth on it.
   ≡   *eyes* ∧

3. Slip ~~yer~~ hand into the sock?.
   your

T19

Name _____

LANGUAGE AND USAGE

RETEACHING WORKBOOK 41

3 | How Something Sounds and Feels

▶ Adjectives tell how something sounds and feels.

> **Sound:** Those trucks are making a **honking** noise.
> **Feel:** They are driving on a **smooth** road.

Write the adjectives that tell how something sounds or feels.

★ Our road was very **bumpy**.
(pink, bumpy)

1. Cars made **loud** noises on it.
(loud, cold)

2. People worked in the **hot** sun.
(big, hot)

3. Tools made **clicking** sounds.
(many, clicking)

4. The **noisy** machines came close to our house.
(noisy, new)

5. The tar felt **sticky** under my feet.
(blue, sticky)

Level 2   Unit 8   Adjectives   (Use with pupil book pages 223–224.)
Skill: Students will write adjectives that describe sound and touch.

Name _____

LANGUAGE AND USAGE

RETEACHING WORKBOOK 40

2 | How Something Tastes and Smells

▶ Adjectives tell how something tastes and smells.

> **Taste:** Lois tastes the **fresh** fish.
> **Smell:** There is a **sweet** smell in the kitchen.

Draw a line under each adjective that tells how something tastes or smells. Then write the sentences.

★ Li's fish tastes (slow, salty).

Li's fish tastes salty.

1. She adds a taste of (soft, sour) lemon.

She adds a taste of sour lemon.

2. Lois likes the potatoes' (peppery, green) taste.

Lois likes the potatoes' peppery taste.

3. Li and Lois smell something (tall, fruity).

Li and Lois smell something fruity.

4. They smell (spicy, round) baked apples.

They smell spicy baked apples.

Level 2   Unit 8   Adjectives   (Use with pupil book pages 221–222.)
Skill: Students will write adjectives that describe taste and smell.

Name _____

Using Exact Words

Use **exact** words to describe something clearly.

A truck <u>has</u> a car.
A truck **pulls** a car.

Write each sentence, using the exact word.

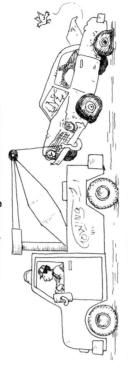

1. Look at that old (thing, car).

   <u>Look at that old car.</u>

2. The front (part, window) is broken.

   <u>The front window is broken.</u>

3. (Two, Some) of the tires are flat.

   <u>Two of the tires are flat.</u>

4. The (stuff, paint) is peeling all over.

   <u>The paint is peeling all over.</u>

Level 2   Unit 9   Description   (Use with pupil book page 248.)
Skill: Students will use exact words in sentences.

Name _____

4 ‖ Adding er and est

▶ Add <u>er</u> to compare two people or things.
▶ Add <u>est</u> to compare more than two people or things.

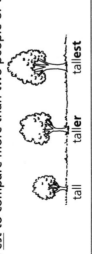

tall   tall**er**   tall**est**

Write the correct word for each sentence.

★ The woods are **quieter** than the street.
   (quieter, quietest)

1. The woods are the **quietest** of all places.
   (quieter, quietest)

2. This tree is **older** than that one.
   (older, oldest)

3. That tree is the **oldest** of all the trees.
   (older, oldest)

4. It is the **tallest** of these three trees.
   (taller, tallest)

Level 2   Unit 8   Adjectives   (Use with pupil book pages 225–226.)
Skill: Students will write the comparative and superlative forms of adjectives.

Step 4: Proofread

	yes
Did I begin and end each sentence correctly?	☐
Did I spell each word correctly?	☐

brother
My ~~brothr~~ is a ℓircus clown⸰?.

Proofreading Marks

∧ Add.

— Take out.

≡ Make a capital letter.

/ Make a small letter.

Proofread these sentences. There are two mistakes in each sentence. Use proofreading marks to correct the mistakes. Use a dictionary to check spellings. Then write each sentence correctly on another piece of paper.

★   has
he ~~hes~~ a silly costume.
≡

He has a silly costume.

1. His face
   His ~~fas~~ is painted ₩hite.

2. ≡his funny nose is soft and round⸰?.

3. His hair is pink and blew.
                              blue

Step 3: Revise

	yes
Have I used exact words?	☐
Have I used details that tell how something looks, sounds, tastes, smells, or feels?	☐

Revise this paragraph. Write an exact word in place of each underlined word. Add a detail to tell how the night looked, sounded, smelled, or felt. Write between the lines.

Sample answers:

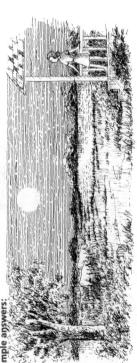

It was a beautiful night. The wind felt nice.
                                     cool ∧

full   Hundreds   stars
The moon was big. Lots of things were shining. I heard
              ∧   ∧

              dashed
A shooting star went across the dark sky. I heard
              ∧

a cow mooing and frogs croaking. fresh
                noises. The air smelled good.
              ∧   ∧

Name _____

MECHANICS

2 | Holidays

▶ Begin the names of holidays with capital letters.

Today is **Father's Day.**

Write the names of the underlined holidays correctly.

★ Does school begin before labor day?

Labor Day

1. We have a picnic on flag day.

   Flag Day

2. Do you go to school on columbus day?

   Columbus Day

3. Grandma will be here on thanksgiving day.

   Thanksgiving Day

4. I gave Dad a card for valentine's day.

   Valentine's Day

5. On presidents' day we saw a parade.

   Presidents' Day

Level 2   Unit 10   Capitalization/Punctuation   *(Use with pupil book pages 265–266.)*
Skill: Students will capitalize the names of holidays.

Name _____

MECHANICS

1 | Days

▶ Use capital letters to begin the names of the days of the week.

Sunday	Tuesday	Thursday	Saturday
Monday	Wednesday	Friday	

Ned will take his piano lesson on **Tuesday.**

Draw a line under the correct word. Then write the sentence correctly.

★ Ned cleans on (friday, <u>Friday</u>).

Ned cleans on Friday.

1. Ned visits Gramps on (<u>Sunday</u>, sunday).

   Ned visits Gramps on Sunday.

2. On (thursday, <u>Thursday</u>) Ned plays soccer.

   On Thursday Ned plays soccer.

3. Ned studies on (<u>Monday</u>, monday).

   Ned studies on Monday.

4. Ned has a picnic on (<u>Saturday</u>, saturday).

   Ned has a picnic on Saturday.

Level 2   Unit 10   Capitalization/Punctuation   *(Use with pupil book pages 263–264.)*
Skill: Students will capitalize the names of the days of the week.

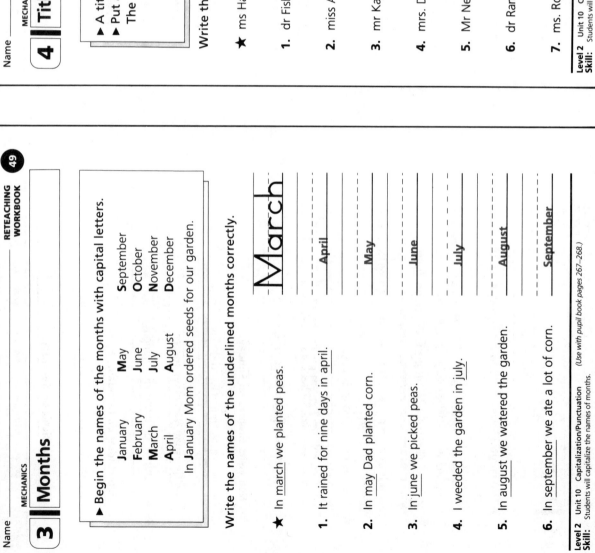

4 Titles for People

▶ A title begins with a capital letter.
▶ Put a period after Mrs., Mr., Ms., and Dr.
The title Miss does not have a period.

Mrs. Perez   **Mr.** Rutter   **Ms.** Chung
            Dr. Finlay   **Miss** Lee

Write the titles and names correctly.

★ ms Hanks

Ms. Hanks

1. dr Fisher

Dr. Fisher

2. miss Allen

Miss Allen

3. mr Kan

Mr. Kan

4. mrs. Dow

Mrs. Dow

5. Mr Nelson

Mr. Nelson

6. dr Ramos

Dr. Ramos

7. ms. Rosen

Ms. Rosen

---

3 Months

▶ Begin the names of the months with capital letters.

January	May	September
February	June	October
March	July	November
April	August	December

In January Mom ordered seeds for our garden.

Write the names of the underlined months correctly.

★ In march we planted peas.

March

1. It rained for nine days in april.

April

2. In may Dad planted corn.

May

3. In june we picked peas.

June

4. I weeded the garden in july.

July

5. In august we watered the garden.

August

6. In september we ate a lot of corn.

September

Worksheet 52:

Name _____

MECHANICS   RETEACHING WORKBOOK   52

6 | Ending Sentences

▶ A telling sentence ends with a period.

Those blue flowers are pretty.

▶ A question ends with a question mark.

Did someone plant them there?

Write the correct end mark for each sentence. Write **Q** after each question. Write **T** after each telling sentence.

★ How do flowers make new plants ___?___ Q

1. Some flowers make seeds ___.___ T

2. Do the seeds fall to the ground ___?___ Q

3. Rain and sun make the seeds grow ___.___ T

4. Do birds carry flower seeds ___?___ Q

5. Birds drop the seeds in new places ___.___ T

6. Do other animals carry seeds ___?___ Q

Level 2   Unit 10   Capitalization/Punctuation   (Use with pupil book pages 273–274.)
Skill: Students will punctuate and will identify statements and questions.

Worksheet 51:

Name _____

MECHANICS   RETEACHING WORKBOOK   51

5 | Writing Book Titles

▶ Begin the first word, the last word, and each important word in a book title with a capital letter. Draw a line under the title.

My favorite book is Make Way for Ducklings.

Write the correct book titles.

★ King of the cats   King of the Cats

King of the Cats

1. One Morning in Maine   one morning in Maine
   One Morning in Maine

2. Whistle for Willie   Whistle for Willie
   Whistle for Willie

3. Green Eggs and ham   Green Eggs and Ham
   Green Eggs and Ham

4. William's Doll   William's Doll
   William's Doll

Level 2   Unit 10   Capitalization/Punctuation   (Use with pupil book pages 271–272.)
Skill: Students will write book titles correctly.

Worksheet 54

8 | Commas with Names of Places

▶ Use a comma between the name of a city and the name of a state.

    Daniel goes to camp in Camden, Maine.

Write each underlined city and state correctly. Put a comma in the correct place.

★ Daniel lives in <u>Detroit Michigan</u>.

Detroit, Michigan

1. Joey comes to camp from <u>Omaha Nebraska</u>.

    Omaha, Nebraska

2. Joey travels through <u>Chicago Illinois</u>.

    Chicago, Illinois

3. Mary comes from <u>Richmond Virginia</u>.

    Richmond, Virginia

4. Mary rides on a train from <u>Baltimore Maryland</u>.

    Baltimore, Maryland

Worksheet 53

7 | Commas in Dates

▶ A date tells a month, a day, and a year.
▶ Use a **comma** , between the day and the year in a date.

    Eva was born February 2, 1982.

Write the correct date.

★ March 7, 1990   March 7 1990

March 7, 1990

1. September, 18 1955   September 18, 1955

    September 18, 1955

2. July 12, 1979   July 12 1979

    July 12, 1979

3. August 4, 1985   August, 4 1985

    August 4, 1985

4. June 28 1983   June 28, 1983

    June 28, 1983

Name _____

COMPOSITION SKILL: LETTERS

Parts of a Letter

Every letter has five parts. The parts are the **date**, the **greeting**, the **body**, the **closing**, and the **name**.

Read this letter. Then write the answers to the questions.

April 25, 1990

Dear Marty,

Our new house is fun. There is a big apple tree in the yard. Can you come for a visit next weekend? We could build a great tree house!

Your friend,
Jessie

1. What is the date? __April 25, 1990__

2. What is the greeting? __Dear Marty,__

3. What is the closing? __Your friend,__

4. Who wrote the letter? __Jessie__

5. Who will receive the letter? __Marty__

Level 2　Unit 11　Letters　(Use with pupil book pages 307–308.)
Skill:　Students will identify the parts of a letter.

Name _____

COMPOSITION SKILL: LETTERS

Kinds of Letters

Some letters say thank you. Some letters tell someone to get well. Invitations ask someone to come to something.

Read the letter below. Then answer the questions.

October 19, 1990

Dear Nita,
Can you come to my birthday party on Saturday? Come to the ice-skating rink at noon.

Your friend,
Mara

1. What kind of letter is this? __invitation__

2. Who will receive the letter? __Nita__

3. Who wrote the letter? __Mara__

4. On what day is the party? __Saturday__

5. What time is the party? __noon__

Level 2　Unit 11　Letters　(Use with pupil book pages 305–306.)
Skill:　Students will identify an invitation.

Step 4: Proofread

	yes
Did I use capital letters correctly?	☐
Did I spell each word correctly?	☐

I got a present in the ~~mal~~ today.

mail

Proofreading Marks

∧ Add.

— Take out.

≡ Make a capital letter.

/ Make a small letter.

Proofread this letter. There are six mistakes. Use proofreading marks to correct the mistakes. Use a dictionary to check spellings. Then write the letter correctly on another piece of paper.

March 16, 1990

Dear Aunt May,

thank y~~ou~~ for the scarf. I love the bright ~~colers~~. I wore it today. I hope that you can come to st~~ae~~ with us soon.

you

colors

stay

Love,

Kristy

Step 3: Revise

	yes
Does my letter tell enough?	☐
Does my letter have all five parts?	☐

Revise Jean's letter. Add two details to make her letter more interesting. Add the missing part to the letter. Write between the lines.

Sample answers:

September 19, 1990

Dear Penny,

I liked seeing you on Saturday ∧ It was good to

at the picnic

meet your friends. I really liked playing with you. ∧

The races were a lot of fun.

hope that we can see each other again soon.

Your friend,
Jean